The Mini Manual of
Cocktails

First published by Parragon in 2010

Parragon

Queen Street House

4 Queen Street

Bath BA1 1HE, UK

Copyright © Parragon Books Ltd 2010

Layout by Stonecastle Graphics Ltd

ISBN 978-1-4075-9364-7

Printed in China

NOTES FOR THE READER

This book uses metric and imperial measurements. Follow the same units of measurement throughout; do not mix metric and imperial. All spoon measurements are level: teaspoons are assumed to be 5 ml and tablespoons are assumed to be 15 ml. Unless otherwise stated, milk is assumed to be full-fat and eggs are medium-size.

WARNING

Recipes using raw or very lightly cooked eggs should be avoided by infants, the elderly, pregnant and breastfeeding women, convalescents and anyone suffering from an illness. Please consume alcohol responsibly.

KEY TO SYMBOLS

★ 'Classic' cocktail

Cocktail or martini glass

Highball glass

Lowball glass

Champagne flute

Wine glass

Shot glass

Brandy snifter

Hurricane glass

Coupette / Margarita glass

Pousse-café glass

Sour glass

The Mini Manual of
Cocktails

Bath · New York · Singapore · Hong Kong · Cologne · Delhi · Melbourne

CONTENTS

Introduction   6

The Classics   16

The New Wave   28

The Perfect Pick-me-up   38

Renaissance   50

Innovative   62

In Vogue   72

Party Starter   84

Layered Lift-off   96

The Perfect Shot   106

Keeping a Clear Head   118

Index   126

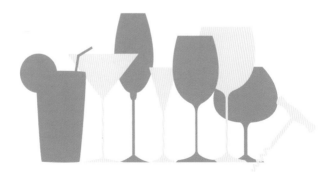

HOW TO USE THE RECIPES

The recipes in this guide have been researched and collated from a wide range of sources. As a result, you'll find that most use measures, but a few use metric and/ or imperial measurements. Unfortunately there are no international standards for bar measures. In Europe a cocktail measure is usually 25 ml or approximately 3/4 fl oz, which is where a jigger makes it easier and an accurate measuring jug is useful, too.

With the measures given in these recipes, it is essentially about the ratio of the base spirit to the modifier, the juice, champagne or cream that holds the drink together and actually turns it into a cocktail. As with any recipe, to get the required result you need to follow the instructions carefully. If the recipe says chill the glass, then chill it. If it tells you to fill the glass with ice, fill it. If it asks for cracked ice, don't use crushed ice. Where the recipe calls for ice other than ordinary ice cubes, then this is specified in the list of ingredients. It's all in the detail, so don't be sloppy.

However, a good bartender will always fine-tune a cocktail and once you've mastered the basic recipe, try substituting one ingredient for a similar one, adjusting the quantities slightly or seeing what effect a different garnish will have. If you taste the resulting cocktails side by side, it will help you develop your own palate and ultimately you'll be able to mix better drinks.

INTRODUCTION

Cocktails may drift in and out of fashion but their appeal is always to the young, or at least the young at heart. Making mixed drinks – even the wonderfully colourful and exotic concoctions of the contemporary cocktail bar – isn't difficult and is great fun. Reading the following basic guidelines should guarantee that you have all the skills of a professional bartender at your fingertips.

GARNISHES

From the classic cocktail cherry or olive through citrus slices, mini fruit kebabs, edible flowers and kitschy accessories if you must, garnishes are part of the cocktail experience and decorating a cocktail is part of the fun.

Garnishes can even contribute to the flavour of a cocktail, particularly when it comes to lemon, orange, lime and even grapefruit peel. For a twist of peel, use a special citrus stripper, vegetable peeler or small sharp knife. Try to remove as much of the white part as possible and cut a piece of skin lengthways. Twist this just above the surface of the drink, rind-side downwards, to release the citrus oil and either hang it on the glass or drop it in. To create a spiral, start at the top of the fruit and work your way around it.

BAR ESSENTIALS

COCKTAIL SHAKER

The standard type is a cylindrical metal container with a capacity of 500 ml/18 fl oz that has a double lid incorporating a perforated strainer. To use, remove the lid, add ice and pour in the ingredients listed in the recipe. Close securely and shake vigorously for 10–20 seconds, until the outside of the shaker is frosted with a fine mist. Remove the small lid and pour the cocktail into the appropriate glass. If your cocktail shaker does not have a built-in strainer, use a separate one. The Boston shaker consists of double conical containers and is designed to be used with a Hawthorn strainer. It's best not to mix more than two servings at a time.

MIXING GLASS

This is used for making clear cocktails. You may use the container of your cocktail shaker or a jug about the same size, but you can also buy a professional mixing glass. To use, add ice, pour in the ingredients and stir for 20 seconds. Strain into the appropriate glass.

STRAINER

A bar strainer or Hawthorn strainer is perfect to prevent ice and other unwanted ingredients from being poured from the shaker or mixing glass into the serving glass. You could also use a small nylon sieve.

JIGGER

This small measuring cup is often double-ended and shaped like an hourglass. Standard metric jiggers are 25 ml and 35 ml while imperial jiggers are 1 fl oz and $1^1/2$ fl oz, representing 1 and $1^1/2$ measures respectively. The proportions of the various ingredients are critical, not the specific quantities, so if you don't have a jigger, you can use the small lid of your cocktail shaker, a liqueur, schnapps or shot glass, or even a small eggcup.

BAR SPOON

This long-handled spoon is used for stirring cocktails in a mixing glass.

MUDDLER

This is simply a miniature masher used for crushing ingredients such as herbs and sugar in the base of a glass. You can also use a mortar and pestle or even the back of a spoon.

OTHER BASICS

Lots of ordinary kitchen equipment is useful: one or more corkscrews, citrus juicer or reamer, chopping board, paring, kitchen and canelle knives, citrus zester, a selection of jugs, measuring cups and a blender for creamy cocktails and slushes. You will also need an ice bucket and tongs – never pick up ice with your fingers. Optional extras include swizzle sticks and straws.

BARTENDER'S TIPS

SUGAR SYRUP

Even fine icing sugar often fails to dissolve completely in the brief time that a cocktail is shaken or stirred, so it is better to use sugar syrup or syrop de gomme when sweetening drinks. To make this, put 4 tablespoons of icing sugar and 4 tablespoons of water into a small saucepan. Gradually bring to the boil over a low heat, stirring constantly until the sugar has dissolved. Boil, without stirring, for 1–2 minutes, then and leave to cool. Store in a sterilized jar or bottle in the refrigerator for up to two months.

CHILLING

For absolute perfection you should chill spirits, mixers and serving glasses in the refrigerator. However, it's not always possible to find room for glasses and you should never put fine crystal in the refrigerator. As an alternative, fill glasses with cracked ice, stir well, then tip out the ice and any water before use.

FROSTING GLASSES

You can use caster sugar, fine salt or desiccated coconut to decorate the rim of a glass. Simply rub the rim with a little lemon or lime juice and then dip the glass upside down into a shallow saucer containing your chosen decoration.

LAYERING (POUSSE-CAFÉ)

To make a multi-layered drink, slowly pour the liqueurs or spirits, in the order specified in the recipe, over the back of a teaspoon into the glass. Each layer then settles on top of the layer before it.

ICE

To crack ice, put cubes in a strong plastic bag and hit with the smooth side of a meat mallet or a rolling pin. Alternatively, bang the bag against a wall. Ice can be crushed in a food processor or blender. To store large quantities of ice, place the cubes in a strong plastic bag and before returning them to the freezer squirt with soda water to stop the cubes from sticking together.

GUIDE TO GLASSES

CLASSIC GLASSWARE

A traditional cocktail glass is sometimes referred to as a martini glass or stem cocktail glass. As with other stemware, the stem allows the drinker to hold the glass without affecting the temperature of the drink. The shape of the glass also helps keep the ingredients from separating. Cocktail glasses are usually used to serve cocktails without ice. They normally hold between 85 ml/3 fl oz and 170 ml/6 fl oz. A variation is the double martini glass, which is taller and wider at the top.

COCKTAIL OR MARTINI GLASS

The most obviously recognizable cocktail glass, the conical martini glass, emerged with the Art Deco movement. It made its debut at the 1925 Paris Exposition of Decorative Arts as a clever twist on the goblet. And like most stemmed glasses – or 'stemware' – this Y-shaped variety proved perfect for chilled cocktails, keeping people's hands from inadvertently warming their drinks. It gained popularity in Europe, particularly for martinis, before proceeding to world domination after World War II.

COUPETTE OR MARGARITA GLASS

Today's Margarita glass is based on the earlier champagne coupe, the saucer-shaped stem glass originally used for serving bubbly. Legend has it the coupe was modelled on a woman's breast. However, it was designed in 1663 so the story that it involved the anatomy of French queen Marie Antoinette must be apocryphal. To facilitate the rimming with salt necessary for Margaritas, the bowl of the coupette was widened. It's also used for Daiquiris.

CHAMPAGNE FLUTE

The tall, thin flute glass has a hazy history. It dates back centuries, with its tapered design reducing the liquid's surface area and keeping champagne bubbling for longer. However, it only became fashionable in the 1950s, possibly after Austrian glassmaker Claus Josef Riedel began researching the way different glass shapes affect taste. Since then, flutes have largely supplanted the coupe for champagne and champagne cocktails – helped by the fact that more flutes fit on a serving tray.

HIGHBALL GLASS

Highball glasses are tall tumblers suitable for simple drinks with a high proportion of mixer to spirit. They're not only an essential component of any home bar, but the title 'highball drinks' also encompasses a host of classic tipples such as bourbon and water, scotch and soda, Bloody Marys and Vodka Tonics. Highball glasses are versatile enough to substitute for the similarly shaped, but slightly larger, Collins glass.

LOWBALL GLASS

The terms 'lowball,' 'rocks' and 'old-fashioned' are bandied around freely when referring to short, squat tumblers. As the second name suggests, they're perfect for holding ice and any spirit 'on the rocks' should be served in one of these. Lowball glasses are also popular for short mixed drinks, such as Old-fashioneds. Variants include the Sazerac glass, named after the cognac and bitters New Orleans cocktail. The double rocks glass, nicknamed 'the bucket', is used for tropical punch-style drinks.

SHOT GLASS

This is the home-bar essential that most frequently moonlights as a novelty collector's item. The regular, unadorned shot glass holds just enough liquid to be downed in a mouthful and boasts a thick base to withstand being slammed on the bar after the neat spirits or mixed-spirits 'shooter' within has been consumed. Standard shot glasses are not just handy for toasts, they can stand in for jiggers too. And decorated with a variety of designs, they've become popular souvenirs.

BRANDY SNIFTER

The brandy snifter stands apart from other stemware. Whereas most stemmed glasses keep warm human hands off chilled drinks, the short-stemmed, bowl-shaped snifter invites you to cradle it in your palm, warming its amber spirit. The wide bottom creates a large surface from which the brandy can evaporate and the aroma is trapped as the glass narrows to a constricted mouth, allowing you to inhale pleasurably before sipping. A snifter should be no more than a third filled.

SOUR GLASS

As one of the oldest family of mixed drinks, unsurprisingly sours have been served up in all manner of glasses, from lowball to martini. Sticklers for style, however, will be pleased to learn that standard drink-ware exists. The glass specified for whisky sours, pisco sours and other citrus, sugar and spirits drinks is a smaller, modified champagne flute – narrow at the stem and widening out at the lip.

HURRICANE GLASS

Most glasses are designed and named for certain drinks, but this isn't exclusively true of the large (775 ml/26 fl oz) hurricane glass. Although originally badged to contain the passion-fruit-and-rum 'Hurricane' cocktail at New Orleans bar Pat O'Brien's, its pear shape is a homage to the hurricane lamp. Today it's associated with frozen and blended cocktails. A frozen Piña Colada is virtually unthinkable without it and it's often used for flamboyantly named cocktails of the Sex-on-the-Beach ilk.

POUSSE-CAFÉ GLASS

These small, narrow-stemmed vessels have a modified hourglass figure, which makes it easier to create layered drinks. Essentially, they're cordial or liqueur glasses, with a flare at the top. Naturally, the art of any layered drink is pouring the heaviest liqueur or syrup first and progressively layering lighter spirits. The bulb shape at the bottom helps trap the lower layers and it's easy to gently drizzle liquids down the sides, thus causing less disturbance to those below.

WINE GLASS

White wine glasses tend to be smaller than red wine glasses, so use your judgment as to which will best accommodate the particular cocktail you are making. If a recipe mentions a goblet, however, go for a red wine glass or even a rounder balloon wine glass.

IRISH COFFEE GLASS

The key feature of an Irish coffee glass is that it's made of heatproof glass, which makes it suitable for hot cocktails such as toddies. It's usually short-stemmed, with a handle, or may have a metal base and handle.

MUG

While not the height of sophistication, a mug is heatproof and is sometimes just what you need for a hot cocktail, especially if it's winter, the event is an outdoor one and guests may be wearing gloves.

TANKARD

Occasionally recipes call for a tankard – traditionally a large, robust, single-handled drinking vessel, commonly made of silver, pewter or glass – but if you don't have one then a standard beer glass is a suitable substitute.

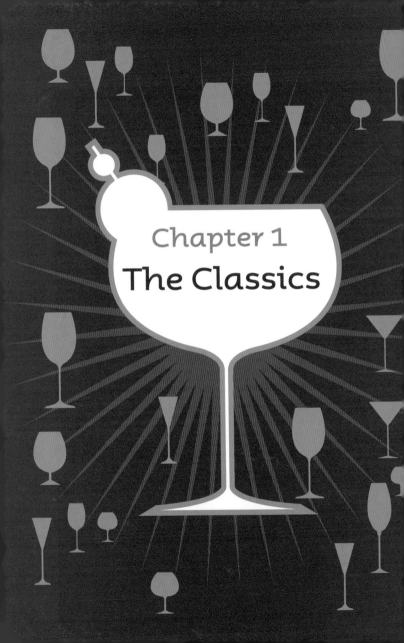

Chapter 1
The Classics

MARTINI

SERVES 1
3 measures gin
1 tsp dry vermouth, or to taste
cracked ice
green cocktail olive, to dress

FOR MANY, THIS IS THE ULTIMATE COCKTAIL. IT IS NAMED AFTER ITS INVENTOR, MARTINI DI ARMA DI TAGGIA, NOT THE FAMOUS BRAND OF VERMOUTH! IT CAN VARY HUGELY, FROM THE ORIGINAL (SEE BELOW) TO THE ULTRA DRY, WHEN THE GLASS IS MERELY RINSED OUT WITH VERMOUTH.

1. Pour the gin and vermouth over cracked ice in a mixing glass and stir well to mix.

2. Strain into a chilled cocktail glass and dress with the cocktail olive.

MANHATTAN

SERVES 1
dash Angostura bitters
3 measures rye whiskey
1 measure sweet vermouth
cracked ice
cocktail cherry, to dress

SAID TO HAVE BEEN INVENTED BY SIR WINSTON CHURCHILL'S AMERICAN MOTHER, JENNIE, THE MANHATTAN IS ONE OF MANY COCKTAILS NAMED AFTER PLACES IN NEW YORK.

1. Shake the liquids over cracked ice in a mixing glass and mix well.

2. Strain into a chilled glass and dress with the cherry.

PIÑA COLADA

SERVES 1
4–6 ice cubes, crushed
2 measures white rum
1 measure dark rum
3 measures pineapple juice
2 measures coconut cream
pineapple wedges, to dress

ONE OF THE YOUNGER GENERATION OF CLASSICS, THIS
BECAME POPULAR DURING THE COCKTAIL REVIVAL OF
THE 1980S AND HAS REMAINED SO EVER SINCE.

1. Whizz the crushed ice in a blender with the white
rum, dark rum, pineapple juice and coconut cream
until smooth.

2. Pour, without straining, into a tall chilled glass and
dress with the pineapple wedges.

MARGARITA

SERVES 1
lime wedge
coarse salt
cracked ice
3 measures white tequila
1 measure triple sec or
    Cointreau
2 measures lime juice
lime wedge, to dress

THIS COCKTAIL, ATTRIBUTED TO FRANCISCO MORALES AND INVENTED IN 1942 IN MEXICO, IS A MORE CIVILIZED VERSION OF THE ORIGINAL WAY TO DRINK TEQUILA – LICK OF SALT FROM THE BACK OF YOUR HAND, SUCK OF LIME JUICE AND A SHOT OF TEQUILA!

1. Rub the rim of a chilled cocktail glass with the lime wedge and then dip in a saucer of coarse salt to frost.

2. Put the cracked ice into a cocktail shaker. Pour the tequila, triple sec and lime juice over the ice. Shake vigorously until a frost forms.

3. Strain into the prepared glass and dress with the lime wedge.

MAI TAI

SERVES 1
2 measures white rum
2 measures dark rum
1 measure orange curaçao
1 measure lime juice
1 tbsp orgeat
1 tbsp grenadine
cracked ice
pineapple slices, fruit peel pieces,
    cocktail cherries, and straws,
    to dress

CREATED IN 1944 BY RESTAURATEUR 'TRADER VIC',
IT WAS DESCRIBED AS 'MAI TAI – ROE AE' MEANING
'OUT OF THIS WORLD'. IT IS ALWAYS FLAMBOYANTLY
DRESSED.

1. Shake the white and dark rums, curaçao, lime juice,
orgeat and grenadine vigorously over ice until well
frosted.

2. Strain into a chilled cocktail glass and dress as
you wish.

SINGAPORE SLING

SERVES 1
2 measures gin
1 measure cherry brandy
1 measure lemon juice
1 tsp grenadine
cracked ice
soda water
lime peel and cocktail
  cherries

1. Shake the gin, cherry brandy, lemon juice and grenadine vigorously over ice until well frosted.

2. Half-fill a chilled glass with cracked ice and strain in the cocktail.

3. Top up with soda water and dress with the lime peel and the cocktail cherries.

MIMOSA

SERVES 1
1 passion fruit
1/2 measure orange
  curaçao
crushed ice
champagne, chilled
star fruit slice, to dress

1. Scoop out the passion fruit flesh into a jug or shaker and shake with the curaçao and a little crushed ice until frosted.

2. Pour into the base of a champagne flute and top up with champagne.

3. Dress with the slice of star fruit.

DRY MARTINI

SERVES 1
1 measure London Dry gin
dash dry vermouth
ice
olive, to dress

1. Shake the gin and vermouth over a handful of ice until well frosted and combined.

2. Strain into a chilled glass.

3. Dress with the olive.

HURRICANE

SERVES 1
ice
4 measures dark rum
1 measure lemon juice
2 measures sweet fruit
   cocktail or juice
   (passion fruit and
   orange are the usual)
soda water
orange slices and
   cherries, to dress

1. Fill a tall cocktail glass or highball glass with ice.

2. Shake the rum, lemon juice and sweet fruit cocktail until well combined and pour into the chilled glass.

3. Top up with soda water and dress with the orange slices and cherries.

CLUB MOJITO

SERVES 1
1 tsp syrop de gomme
few mint leaves, plus extra
    to dress
juice of 1/2 lime
ice
2 measures Jamaican rum
soda water
dash Angostura bitters

★ ⌷ ▌

DARK RUM IS RICH IN FLAVOUR AND REDOLENT OF
SUNNY HOLIDAY MEMORIES.

1. Put the syrup, mint leaves and lime juice in a cocktail
glass and crush or muddle the mint leaves.

2. Add ice and rum, then top up with soda water to
taste.

3. Finish with a dash of Angostura bitters and dress
with the mint leaves.

SANGRIA

SERVES 6
juice of 1 orange
juice of 1 lemon
2 tbsp caster sugar
ice cubes
1 orange, thinly sliced
1 lemon, thinly sliced
1 bottle red wine, chilled
lemonade

A PERFECT LONG COLD DRINK FOR A CROWD OF
FRIENDS AT A SUMMER BARBECUE!

1. Shake the orange juice and lemon juice with the
sugar and transfer to a large bowl or jug.

2. When the sugar has dissolved, add a few ice cubes,
the sliced fruit and wine.

3. Marinate for 1 hour if possible and then add
lemonade to taste and more ice.

DAIQUIRI

SERVES 1
2 measures white rum
3/4 measure lime juice
1/2 tsp sugar syrup
cracked ice

DAIQUIRI IS A TOWN IN CUBA, WHERE THIS DRINK WAS SAID TO HAVE BEEN INVENTED IN THE EARLY PART OF THE TWENTIETH CENTURY.

1. Pour the rum, lime juice and sugar syrup over ice and shake vigorously until well frosted.

2. Strain into a chilled cocktail glass.

BELLINI

SERVES 1
1 measure fresh peach juice
    made from lightly sweetened
    liquidized peaches
caster sugar
3 measures champagne, chilled

THIS DELICIOUS CONCOCTION WAS CREATED BY
GIUSEPPE CIPRIANI AT HARRY'S BAR IN VENICE,
AROUND 1943.

1. Dip the rim of a champagne flute into some peach
juice and then into the sugar to create a sugar-frosted
effect. Set aside to dry.

2. Pour the peach juice into the chilled flute.

3. Carefully top up with champagne.

Chapter 2
The New Wave

MINT JULEP

SERVES 1
leaves from 1 fresh mint sprig, plus
    extra to dress
1 tbsp sugar syrup
crushed ice cubes
3 measures bourbon whiskey

A JULEP IS SIMPLY A MIXED DRINK SWEETENED WITH
SYRUP. THE MINT JULEP IS THE TRADITIONAL DRINK
OF THE KENTUCKY DERBY – THE FIRST LEG OF THE US
TRIPLE CROWN OF HORSE RACING.

1. Put the mint leaves and sugar syrup into a small
chilled glass and mash with a teaspoon.

2. Add the crushed ice and shake to mix before adding
the bourbon.

3. Dress with the mint sprig.

WHITE LADY

SERVES 1
2 measures gin
1 measure triple sec
1 measure lemon juice
cracked ice

SIMPLE, ELEGANT, SUBTLE AND MUCH MORE POWERFUL THAN APPEARANCE SUGGESTS, THIS IS THE PERFECT COCKTAIL TO SERVE BEFORE AN AL FRESCO SUMMER DINNER.

1. Shake the gin, triple sec and lemon juice vigorously over ice until well frosted.

2. Strain into a chilled cocktail glass.

KAMIKAZE

SERVES 1
1 measure vodka
1 measure triple sec
1/2 measure fresh lime juice
1/2 measure fresh lemon juice
ice
dry white wine, chilled
cucumber slices, to dress

NO TURNING BACK ON THIS ONE. IT'S SO DELICIOUS –
YOU WON'T BE ABLE TO PUT IT DOWN.

1. Shake the vodka, triple sec, lime juice and lemon
juice together over ice until well frosted.

2. Strain into a chilled glass and top up with wine.

3. Dress with the slices of cucumber.

BLACK WIDOW

SERVES 1
2/3 measure dark rum
1/3 measure Southern Comfort
juice 1/2 lime
dash curaçao
ice
soda water
lime peel twist, to dress

NOT AS WICKED AS ITS TITLE SUGGESTS, BUT IF YOU ARE FEELING ADVENTUROUS YOU COULD DRINK IT NEAT, ON THE ROCKS!

1. Shake together the rum, Southern Comfort, lime juice and curaçao over ice until well mixed and strain into a chilled tumbler.

2. Top up with soda water to taste and dress with the twist of lime peel.

NIRVANA

SERVES 1
2 measures dark rum
1/2 measure grenadine
1/2 measure tamarind syrup
1 tsp sugar syrup
ice and cracked ice
grapefruit juice

IT MAY NOT BE POSSIBLE TO OBTAIN A PERFECT STATE OF HARMONY AND BLISS THROUGH A COCKTAIL, BUT THIS HAS TO BE THE NEXT BEST THING.

1. Shake the rum, grenadine, tamarind syrup and sugar syrup vigorously over ice until well frosted.

2. Half-fill a chilled glass with cracked ice and strain the cocktail over them.

3. Top up with grapefruit juice.

MUDSLIDE

SERVES 1
1¹/₂ measures Kahlúa
1¹/₂ measures Baileys
   Irish Cream
1¹/₂ measures vodka
cracked ice

1. Shake the Kahlúa, Baileys Irish Cream and vodka vigorously over ice until well frosted.

2. Strain into a chilled glass.

ISLAND BLUES

SERVES 1
lemon juice
caster sugar
³/₄ measure peach
   schnapps
¹/₂ measure blue curaçao
1 small egg white
dash fresh lemon juice
ice
lemonade

1. Frost the rim of a glass using the lemon juice and sugar. Set aside to dry.

2. Place the peach schnapps, blue curaçao, egg white and lemon juice into a cocktail shaker half full of ice.

3. Shake well and strain into a glass.

4. Top up with lemonade.

OCEAN BREEZE

SERVES 1
1 measure white rum
1 measure amaretto
1/2 measure blue curaçao
1/2 measure pineapple
   juice
crushed ice
soda water

1. Shake the white rum, amaretto, blue curaçao and pineapple juice together over ice.

2. Pour into a tall glass and top up with soda water to taste.

INDIAN SUMMER

SERVES 1
1 measure vodka
2 measures Kahlúa
1 measure gin
2 measures pineapple
   juice
ice
tonic water

1. Shake the vodka, Kahlúa, gin and pineapple juice together over ice until frosted.

2. Strain into a medium cocktail glass or wine glass and top up with tonic water to taste.

PALM BEACH

SERVES 1
1 measure white rum
1 measure gin
1 measure pineapple juice
cracked ice

IF IT'S BEEN A LONG TIME SINCE YOUR LAST HOLIDAY, CONJURE UP THE BLUE SKIES AND THE ROLLING SURF OF FLORIDA WITH THIS SUNNY COCKTAIL.

1. Shake the rum, gin and pineapple juice vigorously over ice until well frosted.

2. Strain into a chilled glass.

WHISKY SOUR

SERVES 1
1 measure lemon or lime juice
2 measures blended whisky
1 tsp caster sugar or sugar syrup
ice
lime or lemon slice, to dress
maraschino cherry, to dress

ORIGINATING IN THE SOUTH OF THE USA AND USING SOME OF THE BEST AMERICAN WHISKY, THIS CLASSIC CAN ALSO BE MADE WITH VODKA, GIN OR OTHER SPIRITS.

1. Shake the lemon juice, whisky and sugar together over ice and strain into a cocktail glass.

2. Dress with the slice of lime or lemon and the cherry.

Chapter 3
The Perfect
Pick-me-up

ZOMBIE

SERVES 1
2 measures dark rum
2 measures white rum
1 measure golden rum
1 measure triple sec
1 measure lime juice
1 measure orange juice
1 measure pineapple juice
1 measure guava juice
1 tbsp grenadine
1 tbsp orgeat syrup
1 tsp Pernod
crushed ice cubes
fresh mint sprigs and pineapple
    wedges, to dress

THE INDIVIDUAL INGREDIENTS OF THIS COCKTAIL,
INCLUDING LIQUEURS AND FRUIT JUICES, VARY
CONSIDERABLY FROM ONE RECIPE TO ANOTHER, BUT
ALL ZOMBIES CONTAIN A MIXTURE OF WHITE, GOLDEN
AND DARK RUM IN A RANGE OF PROPORTIONS.

1. Shake all the liquids together over crushed ice until
well combined and frosted.

2. Pour without straining into a chilled glass.

3. Dress with the mint and wedges of pineapple.

WHITE COSMOPOLITAN

SERVES 1
1¹/₂ measures Limoncello
¹/₂ measure Cointreau
1 measure white cranberry and
    grape juice
ice
dash orange bitters
few red cranberries, to dress

NOTHING LIKE ITS PINK COUSIN THE COSMOPOLITAN,
FOR THIS IS FAR MORE FRUITY AND INSTEAD OF
VODKA, IT IS BASED ON A PUNCHY LEMON-
FLAVOURED LIQUEUR.

1. Shake the Limoncello, Cointreau and cranberry and
grape juice over ice until well frosted.

2. Strain into a chilled glass.

3. Add a dash of bitters and dress with the cranberries.

THE BLUES

SERVES 1
1 1/2 measures tequila
1/2 measure maraschino liqueur
1/2 measure blue curaçao
1/2 measure lemon juice
ice cubes
bitter lemon

THIS BRIGHT COCKTAIL WOULD BE QUITE SWEET IF IT WEREN'T FOR THE LEMON JUICE, SO BE CAREFUL WITH THE BALANCE OF THE INGREDIENTS THE FIRST TIME YOU MAKE IT.

1. Shake the tequila, maraschino liqueur, blue curaçao and lemon juice together over ice until frosted.

2. Strain into a tumbler and top up with bitter lemon.

CHARLESTON

SERVES 1
¼ measure gin
¼ measure dry vermouth
¼ measure sweet vermouth
¼ measure Cointreau
¼ measure Kirsch
¼ measure maraschino liqueur
ice
lemon peel twist, to dress

THIS LITTLE NUMBER COMBINES SEVERAL TASTES AND FLAVOURS TO PRODUCE A VERY LIVELY DRINK. DON'T DRINK IT WHEN YOU ARE THIRSTY, OR YOU MIGHT WANT TOO MANY!

1. Shake all the liquids together well over ice and strain into a chilled glass.

2. Dress with the twist of lemon peel.

PINK SQUIRREL

SERVES 1
2 measures dark crème de cacao
1 measure crème de noyaux
1 measure single cream
cracked ice

CRÈME DE NOYAUX HAS A WONDERFUL, SLIGHTLY
BITTER, NUTTY FLAVOUR, BUT IS, IN FACT, MADE FROM
PEACH AND APRICOT KERNELS. IT IS USUALLY SERVED
AS A LIQUEUR, BUT DOES COMBINE WELL WITH SOME
OTHER INGREDIENTS IN COCKTAILS.

1. Shake the crème de cacao, crème de noyaux and
single cream vigorously over ice until well frosted.

2. Strain into a chilled glass.

ZANDER

SERVES 1
1 measure sambuca
1 measure orange juice
dash lemon juice
ice
bitter lemon

1. Shake the sambuca, orange juice and lemon juice vigorously over ice and strain into a glass filled with ice.

2. Top up with bitter lemon.

MOONLIGHT

SERVES 4
3 measures grapefruit
   juice
4 measures gin
1 measure Kirsch
4 measures white wine
1/2 tsp lemon zest
ice

1. Shake all the ingredients together over ice and strain into chilled glasses.

ORANGE BLOSSOM

SERVES 1
2 measures gin
2 measures orange juice
cracked ice
orange slice, to dress

1. Shake the gin and orange juice vigorously over ice until well frosted.

2. Strain into a chilled cocktail glass and dress with the slice of orange.

APPLE CLASSIC

SERVES 1
1/2 measure gin
1/2 measure brandy
1/2 measure Calvados
ice
sweet cider
apple slice, to dress

1. Shake the gin, brandy and Calvados over ice until frosted.

2. Strain into a medium or tall glass and top up with cider to taste.

3. Dress with the slice of apple.

DEAUVILLE PASSION

SERVES 1
1³/4 measures cognac
1¹/4 measures apricot curaçao
1¹/4 measures passion fruit juice
ice
bitter lemon, to taste
mint leaves, to dress

DEAUVILLE WAS ELEGANT, EXTRAVAGANT AND VERY
FASHIONABLE DURING THE COCKTAIL ERA EARLY LAST
CENTURY AND NO DOUBT MANY GREAT COCKTAILS
WERE CREATED THERE.

1. Shake the cognac, apricot curaçao and passion fruit
juice over ice until well frosted.

2. Strain into a chilled glass, top with the bitter lemon
and dress with the mint leaves.

ADAM AND EVE

SERVES 1
2 measures triple sec
1 measure vodka
1 measure grapefruit juice
1 measure cranberry juice
ice
5–6 pineapple cubes
2 tsp caster sugar
crushed ice
strawberry slice, to dress

DON'T EXPECT THIS COCKTAIL TO BE FULL OF APPLES!
THE BASE IS SHARP AND ASTRINGENT, WHILE THE TOP
IS SWEET AND FROTHY – NO DISCRIMINATION HERE,
OF COURSE!

1. Shake the triple sec, vodka, grapefruit juice and
cranberry juice over ice until well frosted.

2. Strain into a chilled glass.

3. In a blender whizz the pineapple with the sugar and
1–2 tbsp of crushed ice to a frothy slush.

4. Float gently on the top of the cocktail.

5. Dress with the slice of strawberry.

CHERRY KITCH

SERVES 1
1 measure cherry brandy
2 measures pineapple juice
1/2 measure Kirsch
1 egg white
crushed ice
frozen maraschino cherry,
    to dress

THIS IS A VELVETY SMOOTH COCKTAIL, FRUITY BUT
WITH A RICH BRANDY UNDERTONE. A TOUCH OF
MARASCHINO LIQUEUR ADDED AT THE END WOULD BE
GOOD TOO.

1. Shake the cherry brandy, pineapple juice, Kirsch and
egg white over ice until frosted.

2. Pour into a chilled tall thin glass and top with the
frozen maraschino cherry.

MARTINEZ

SERVES 1
2 measures iced gin
1 measure Italian
    vermouth
dash Angostura bitters
dash maraschino liqueur
ice cubes
lemon twist or slice

THE ORIGINAL RECIPE MAY GO BACK TO 1849 AND
WAS MADE WITH A GIN CALLED OLD TOM THAT WAS
SLIGHTLY SWEETENED.

1. Shake the gin, vermouth, Angostura bitters and
maraschino liqueur over ice until frosted.

2. Strain into a chilled cocktail glass and dress with the
twist of lemon.

Chapter 4
Renaissance

COSMOPOLITAN

SERVES 1
2 measures vodka
1 measure triple sec
1 measure fresh lime juice
1 measure cranberry juice
ice
orange peel strip, to dress

THIS FASHIONABLE COCKTAIL, MADE FAMOUS BY THE TV SHOW 'SEX AND THE CITY', IS THE ONLY DRINK TO SERVE AT A TRENDY PARTY!

1. Shake all the liquid ingredients over ice until well frosted.

2. Strain into a chilled cocktail glass.

3. Dress with the strip of orange peel.

SEX ON THE BEACH

SERVES 1
1 measure peach schnapps
1 measure vodka
2 measures fresh orange juice
3 measures cranberry and peach
   juice
ice and crushed ice
dash of lemon juice
orange peel piece, to dress

HOLIDAY DRINKS ARE OFTEN LONG AND FRUITY AND
THIS REFRESHING COCKTAIL IS REMINISCENT OF HAPPY
DAYS IN THE SUN.

1. Shake the peach schnapps, vodka, orange juice and
cranberry and peach juice over ice until well frosted.

2. Strain into a glass filled with crushed ice and squeeze
on the lemon juice.

3. Dress with the orange peel.

BLOODY MARY

SERVES 1
dash Worcestershire sauce
dash Tabasco sauce
cracked ice
2 measures vodka
splash dry sherry
6 measures of tomato juice
juice of ¹/₂ lemon
celery salt
cayenne pepper
celery stalk with leaves, to dress
lemon slice, to dress

THIS CLASSIC COCKTAIL WAS INVENTED IN 1921 AT THE LEGENDARY HARRY'S BAR IN PARIS. THERE ARE NUMEROUS VERSIONS – SOME MUCH HOTTER AND SPICIER THAN OTHERS.

1. Dash the Worcestershire sauce and Tabasco sauce over ice in a shaker and add the vodka, splash of dry sherry, tomato juice and lemon juice.

2. Shake vigorously until frosted.

3. Strain into a tall chilled glass, add the pinch of celery salt and the pinch of cayenne and dress with the celery stalk and the slice of lemon.

SCREWDRIVER

SERVES 1
cracked ice
2 measures vodka
orange juice
orange slice, to dress

★ ▮

THIS COCKTAIL HAS UNIVERSAL APPEAL AND IS GREAT
TO SERVE TO GUESTS AT A PARTY IF YOU ARE NOT SURE
OF INDIVIDUAL TASTES. FRESHLY SQUEEZED ORANGE
JUICE IS A MUST.

1. Fill a chilled glass with cracked ice.

2. Pour the vodka over the ice and top up with orange
juice.

3. Stir well to mix and dress with the slice of orange.

BLUE LAGOON

SERVES 1
1 measure blue curaçao
1 measure vodka
dash fresh lemon juice
lemonade

LET YOUR IMAGINATION CARRY YOU AWAY WHILE YOU SINK INTO THIS LUXURIOUSLY BLUE COCKTAIL. IT HAS A REFRESHING LEMON ZING AND SPARKLE TOO.

1. Pour the blue curaçao into a highball or cocktail glass, followed by the vodka.

2. Add the lemon juice and top up with lemonade to taste.

SLOW COMFORTABLE SCREW

SERVES 1
2 measures sloe gin
orange juice
cracked ice
orange slice, to dress

1. Shake the sloe gin and orange juice over ice until well frosted and pour into a chilled glass.

2. Dress with the slice of orange.

HARVEY WALLBANGER

SERVES 1
ice cubes
3 measures vodka
8 measures orange
    juice
2 tsp Galliano
cherry and orange slice,
    to dress

1. Half-fill a tall glass with ice, pour the vodka and orange juice over the ice cubes and float Galliano on top.

2. Dress with the cherry and slice of orange.

3. For a warming variant, mix a splash of ginger wine with the vodka and orange.

JAPANESE SLIPPER

SERVES 1
cracked ice
1 1/2 measures vodka
1 1/2 measures Midori
1 measure freshly
    squeezed lime juice
lime slice, to dress

1. Put the cracked ice into a cocktail shaker and pour in the vodka, Midori and lime juice.

2. Cover and shake vigorously for 10–20 seconds, until the outside of the shaker is misted.

3. Strain into a cocktail glass and dress with the lime slice.

LONG ISLAND ICED TEA

SERVES 1
2 measures vodka
1 measure gin
1 measure white
    tequila
1 measure white rum
1/2 measure white
    crème de menthe
2 measures lemon juice
1 tsp sugar syrup
cracked ice
cola
lime or lemon wedge,
    to dress

1. Shake the vodka, gin, tequila, rum, crème de menthe, lemon juice and sugar syrup vigorously over ice until well frosted.

2. Strain into an ice-filled tall glass and top up with cola.

3. Dress with the wedge of lime or lemon.

BLACK RUSSIAN

SERVES 1
2 measures vodka
1 measure coffee liqueur
4–6 ice cubes, cracked

HISTORY RECORDS ONLY WHITE AND RED RUSSIANS. THE OMISSION OF THE BLACK RUSSIAN IS A SAD OVERSIGHT. FOR A COFFEE LIQUEUR, YOU CAN USE EITHER TIA MARIA OR KAHLÚA.

1. Pour the vodka and liqueur over the cracked ice in a small chilled glass.

2. Stir to mix.

ANOUCHKA

SERVES 1
1 measure vodka, iced
dash black sambuca
dash crème de mure
a few blackberries, fresh or
    frozen, to dress

SAMBUCA IS LICORICE-FLAVOURED AND THEREFORE
NOT TO EVERYONE'S TASTE. HOWEVER, USED HERE
WITH A DASH OF BLACKBERRY LIQUEUR AND THE ICED
VODKA, IT'S A GREAT COMBINATION.

1. Pour the vodka into a chilled shot glass.

2. Add the sambuca and crème de mure.

3. Dress with the blackberries.

GODMOTHER

SERVES 1
4–6 ice cubes, cracked
2 measures vodka
1 measure amaretto

AMARETTO IS AN ITALIAN LIQUEUR, SO PERHAPS
THE INSPIRATION FOR THIS COCKTAIL COMES FROM
DON CORLEONE, THE PROTAGONIST IN MARIO PUZO'S
BEST-SELLING NOVEL.

1. Put the cracked ice into a small chilled tumbler.

2. Pour the vodka and amaretto over the ice.

3. Stir to mix.

RUSSIAN DOUBLE

SERVES 1
1 measure red vodka, iced
lemon or orange peel strips
1 measure lemon vodka
    or schnapps, iced

VODKA AND SCHNAPPS ARE BOTH VERY STRONG
DRINKS, SO HANDLE WITH CARE!

1. Layer the ingredients carefully in a chilled shot
glass, putting the strips of peel in the first layer. Drink
immediately.

Chapter 5
Innovative

BELLINITINI

SERVES 1
2 measures vodka
1 measure peach schnapps
1 measure peach juice
ice
champagne, chilled

A LOVELY VARIATION ON ONE OF THE BEST-KNOWN
APERITIFS – JUST PEACHY.

1. Shake the vodka, peach schnapps and peach juice
vigorously with ice until well frosted.

2. Strain into a chilled and frosted champagne flute.

3. Top up with chilled champagne.

BLACK BEAUTY

SERVES 1
2 measures vodka
1 measure black sambuca
ice
black olive, to dress

FOR A VERY DIFFERENT VERSION, TRY IT WITH ONE OF THE BLACK VODKAS THAT HAVE RECENTLY APPEARED ON THE MARKET. THE DRAMATIC COLOUR AND SUBTLE FLAVOUR ARE WORTH EXPERIENCING.

1. Stir the vodka and sambuca with ice in a mixing glass until frosted.

2. Strain into an iced martini glass and add the olive.

BLUE MONDAY

SERVES 1
cracked ice
1 measure vodka
½ measure Cointreau
1 tbsp blue curaçao

THE LOVELY COLOUR AND FRUITY FLAVOUR OF THIS
COCKTAIL IS GUARANTEED TO MAKE MONDAY YOUR
FAVOURITE DAY OF THE WEEK.

1. Put the cracked ice into a mixing glass or jug and
pour in the vodka, Cointreau and curaçao. Stir well and
strain into a cocktail glass.

MOSCOW MULE

SERVES 1
2 measures vodka
1 measure lime juice
cracked ice
ginger beer
lime slice, to dress

★ ▮

AN AMERICAN BAR OWNER HAD OVERSTOCKED
GINGER BEER AND A REPRESENTATIVE OF A SOFT
DRINKS COMPANY INVENTED THE MOSCOW MULE
TO HELP HIM OUT.

1. Shake the vodka and lime juice vigorously over ice
until well frosted.

2. Half-fill a chilled tall glass with cracked ice and
strain the cocktail over them.

3. Top up with the ginger beer. Dress with the slice
of lime.

PEARTINI

SERVES 1
1 tsp caster sugar
pinch of ground cinnamon
1 lemon wedge
cracked ice
1 measure vodka
1 measure pear brandy, such as
    Poire William or Pera Segnana

WHILE LESS POPULAR THAN PEACH OR CHERRY EAU DE
VIE, PEAR BRANDY HAS A DELICATE FRAGRANCE AND
LOVELY FLAVOUR, BUT DON'T CONFUSE IT WITH PEAR
LIQUEUR.

1. Combine the sugar and cinnamon on a saucer. Rub
the outside rim of a cocktail glass with the lemon
wedge, then dip it into the sugar and cinnamon
mixture. Set aside.

2. Put the cracked ice into a mixing glass or jug and
pour in the vodka and pear brandy. Stir well and strain
into the prepared glass, without disturbing the frosting.

FUZZY NAVEL

SERVES 1
2 measures vodka
1 measure peach
    schnapps
250ml/9 fl oz orange
    juice
cracked ice
physalis (cape gooseberry),
    to dress

1. Shake the vodka, peach schnapps and orange juice vigorously over cracked ice until well frosted.

2. Strain into a chilled cocktail glass and dress with the physalis.

SPOTTED BIKINI

SERVES 1
1 ripe passion fruit
2 measures vodka
1 measure white rum
1 measure cold milk
juice 1/2 lemon
ice
lemon peel slice, to dress

1. Scoop out the passion fruit flesh into a jug.

2. Shake the vodka, white rum, milk and lemon juice over ice until well frosted.

3. Strain into a chilled cocktail glass and add the passion fruit, not strained, at the last minute so you see the black seeds.

4. Dress with the piece of lemon.

GOLDEN FROG

SERVES 1
ice cubes
1 measure vodka
1 measure Strega
1 measure Galliano
1 measure lemon juice

1. Blend 4–6 ice cubes in a blender with the vodka, Strega, Galliano and lemon juice until slushy.

2. Pour into a chilled cocktail glass.

STRAWBERRINI

SERVES 1
4 small fresh or frozen strawberries
1 tbsp caster sugar
1–2 drops fresh lime juice
dash fraise liqueur
2 measures vodka, well iced

1. Reserve a strawberry to add later.

2. Crush the rest in a bowl with the sugar, lime juice and fraise liqueur.

3. Strain well.

4. Pour the vodka into an iced martini glass and add the purée and reserved strawberry.

SALTY DOG

SERVES 1
1 tbsp granulated sugar
1 tbsp coarse salt
lemon half
6–8 ice cubes, cracked
2 measures vodka
grapefruit juice

WHEN THIS COCKTAIL FIRST APPEARED, GIN-BASED MIXES WERE BY FAR THE MOST POPULAR, BUT NOWADAYS A SALTY DOG IS MORE FREQUENTLY MADE WITH VODKA.

1. Mix the sugar and salt in a saucer. Rub the rim of a chilled cocktail glass with the lemon half, then dip it in the sugar and salt mixture to frost.

2. Fill the glass with cracked ice and pour the vodka over them.

3. Top up with grapefruit juice and stir to mix. Drink with a straw.

WOO-WOO

SERVES 1
cracked ice
2 measures vodka
2 measures peach schnapps
4 measures cranberry juice
physalis (cape gooseberry),
    to dress

BE SURE TO WOO YOUR FRIENDS WITH THIS
REFRESHING AND SIMPLE DRINK. IT'S ALSO GREAT
FOR PARTIES.

1. Half-fill a chilled cocktail glass with cracked ice.

2. Pour the vodka, peach schnapps and cranberry juice
over the ice.

3. Stir well to mix and dress with the physalis.

Chapter 6
In Vogue

METROPOLITAN

SERVES 1
1 lemon wedge
1 tbsp caster sugar
cracked ice
1/2 measure vodka or lemon
   vodka
1/2 measure framboise or other
   raspberry liqueur
1/2 measure cranberry juice
1/2 measure orange juice
2 cranberries, to dress

THIS SOPHISTICATED COCKTAIL FOR CITY SLICKERS
SHARES ITS NAME, BUT NOT ITS INGREDIENTS, WITH AN
EQUALLY URBANE CLASSIC FROM THE PAST.

1. Rub the outside rim of a cocktail glass with the lemon
wedge and dip it into the sugar to frost. Set aside.

2. Put the cracked ice into a cocktail shaker and pour
in the vodka, liqueur, cranberry juice and orange juice.
Cover and shake vigorously for 10–20 seconds, until the
outside of the shaker is misted.

3. Strain into the prepared glass, taking care not to
disturb the frosting, and dress with the cranberries.

VODKATINI

SERVES 1
1 measure vodka
ice
dash dry vermouth
lemon peel twist,
 to dress

THE CELEBRATED 007 POPULARIZED THE USE OF
VODKA AS THE BASE OF THE MARTINI, RATHER THAN
GIN, HENCE THE VODKATINI IS NOW WIDELY ACCEPTED
AS AN INCREDIBLY STYLISH AND TASTY ALTERNATIVE.

1. Pour the vodka over a handful of ice in a mixing
glass.

2. Add the vermouth, stir well and strain into a cocktail
glass.

3. Dress with the twist of lemon peel.

VODKA ESPRESSO

SERVES 1
cracked ice
2 measures espresso or
    other strong brewed
    coffee, cooled
1 measure vodka
2 tsp caster sugar
1 measure Amarula

THIS MAKES FOR A FABULOUS AFTER-DINNER TREAT.
IT'S USUALLY MADE WITH STOLICHNAYA VODKA AND
AMARULA, A SOUTH AFRICAN CREAM LIQUEUR WITH A
CARAMEL FLAVOUR.

1. Put the cracked ice into a cocktail shaker, pour in the
coffee and vodka and add the sugar.

2. Cover and shake vigorously for 10–20 seconds, until
the outside of the shaker is misted.

3. Strain into a cocktail glass, then float the Amarula
on top.

FLYING GRASSHOPPER

SERVES 1
cracked ice
1 measure vodka
1 measure green crème
    de menthe
1 measure white crème
    de menthe

THERE ARE TWO VERSIONS OF THIS COCKTAIL – ONE
MADE WITH EQUAL QUANTITIES OF WHITE AND GREEN
CRÈME DE MENTHE AND THIS ONE WITH GREEN CRÈME
DE MENTHE AND CHOCOLATE LIQUEUR.

1. Put the cracked ice into a mixing glass or jug and
pour in the vodka and crème de menthe. Stir well and
strain into a cocktail glass.

PURPLE PASSION

SERVES 1
cracked ice
2 measures vodka
4 measures grapefruit
    juice
4 measures purple grape
    juice
ice cubes

THIS FRUITY COOLER STILL HAS QUITE A KICK AT ITS
HEART. TRY USING ONE OF THE CITRUS-FLAVOURED
VODKAS FOR A SUBTLE CHANGE IN TASTE.

1. Put the cracked ice into a cocktail shaker and pour in
the vodka, grapefruit juice and grape juice.

2. Cover and shake vigorously for 10–20 seconds, until
the outside of the cocktail shaker is misted.

3. Put the ice cubes into a chilled glass and strain the
cocktail over them.

MIMI

SERVES 1
2 measures vodka
1/2 measure coconut
  cream
2 measures pineapple
  juice
crushed ice
fresh pineapple slice or
  fan, to dress

1. Whizz the vodka, coconut cream, pineapple juice and crushed ice in a blender for a few seconds until frothy.

2. Pour into a chilled cocktail glass and dress with the piece of pineapple.

GREYHOUND

SERVES 1
ice cubes
1 1/2 measures vodka or
  lemon vodka
150 ml/5 fl oz freshly
  squeezed grapefruit
  juice

1. Put the ice cubes in a tall glass and pour in the vodka and grapefruit juice. Stir well.

CHOCOLATE MARTINI

SERVES 1
2 measures vodka
¼ measure crème de cacao
2 dashes orange flower water
ice
cocoa powder

1. Shake the vodka, crème de cacao and orange flower water over ice until really well frosted.

2. Strain into a martini glass rimmed with cocoa powder.

APPLE MARTINI

SERVES 1
cracked ice
1 measure vodka
1 measure sour apple schnapps
1 measure apple juice
2 thin apple slices to dress

1. Put the cracked ice into a cocktail shaker and pour in the vodka, schnapps and apple juice.

2. Cover and shake vigorously for 10–20 seconds, until the outside of the shaker is misted.

3. Strain into a cocktail glass and dress with the apple slices.

BULLSHOT

SERVES 1
1 measure vodka
2 measures beef consommé or
    good stock
dash fresh lemon juice
2 dashes Worcestershire sauce
ice
celery salt
lemon peel strip, to dress

THIS IS NOT UNLIKE DRINKING CHILLED CONSOMMÉ –
BUT WITH A NOTICEABLE KICK. IT IS BEST REALLY COLD.

1. Shake all the liquid ingredients together with the ice
and strain into a glass with extra ice.

2. Sprinkle with celery salt and dress with the strip of
lemon peel.

FLIRTINI

SERVES 1
1/4 slice fresh pineapple, chopped
1/2 measure chilled Cointreau
1/2 measure chilled vodka
1 measure chilled pineapple
    juice
chilled champagne or sparkling
    white wine

THIS COMBINATION OF VODKA AND CHAMPAGNE
IS GUARANTEED TO BRING A SPARKLE TO THE EYES
AND A SMILE TO THE LIPS – WHAT COULD BE MORE
ATTRACTIVE?

1. Put the pineapple and Cointreau into a mixing
glass or jug and muddle with a spoon to crush the
pineapple.

2. Add the vodka and pineapple juice and stir well,
then strain into a glass. Top up with champagne.

CRANBERRY COLLINS

SERVES 1
2 measures vodka
3/4 measure elderflower cordial
3 measures white cranberry and
    apple juice or to taste
ice
soda water
cranberries and slice of lime,
    to dress

THE CLASSIC COLLINS DRINK IS MADE WITH GIN, BUT ITS MANY VARIATIONS ARE MADE WITH OTHER SPIRITS, SO TRY THIS ONE ON FOR SIZE.

1. Shake the vodka, elderflower cordial and cranberry and apple juice over ice until well frosted.

2. Strain into a highball glass with more ice and top up with soda water to taste.

3. Dress with the cranberries and the slice of lime.

SILVER BERRY

SERVES 1
1 measure raspberry vodka, iced
1 measure creme de cassis, iced
1 measure Cointreau, iced
edible silver paper or a frozen berry,
  to dress

THIS DRINK IS PERFECT FOR ONE OF THOSE VERY
SPECIAL OCCASIONS – EXCEPT THAT YOU REALLY
CAN'T DRINK VERY MANY!

1. Carefully and slowly layer the three liquors in
the order listed, in a well-iced shot glass or tall thin
cocktail glass. They must be well iced first and may
need time to settle into their layers.

2. Dress with the silver paper or a frozen berry.

Chapter 7
Party Starter

BRAIN HAEMORRHAGE

SERVES 1
1 measure chilled peach schnapps
1 tsp chilled Baileys Irish Cream
1/2 tsp chilled grenadine

THIS IS A RARE INSTANCE OF A COCKTAIL THAT IS DELIBERATELY INTENDED TO LOOK HORRID, RATHER THAN TEMPTING AND WAS PROBABLY INVENTED TO DRINK AT HALLOWEEN.

1. Pour the peach schnapps into a shot glass, then carefully float the Baileys on top. Finally, top with the grenadine.

TEQUILA SLAMMER

SERVES 1
1 measure white tequila, chilled
1 measure lemon juice
sparkling wine, chilled

SLAMMERS ARE ALSO KNOWN AS SHOOTERS. THE IDEA IS THAT YOU POUR THE INGREDIENTS INTO THE GLASS, WITHOUT STIRRING. COVER THE GLASS WITH ONE HAND TO PREVENT SPILLAGE, SLAM IT ON TO A TABLE TO MIX AND DRINK!

1. Put the tequila and lemon juice into a chilled glass.

2. Top up with sparkling wine.

3. Cover the glass with your hand and slam.

ALABAMA SLAMMER

SERVES 1
1 measure Southern Comfort
1 measure amaretto
1/2 measure sloe gin
cracked ice
1/2 tsp lemon juice

SMALL, BUT PERFECTLY PROPORTIONED – THIS IS A
SHOOTER WITH A REAL KICK!

1. Pour the Southern Comfort, amaretto and sloe gin
over cracked ice in a mixing glass and stir.

2. Strain into a shot glass and add the lemon juice.

3. Cover and slam.

HIGH FLYER

SERVES 1
²/₃ measure gin
¹/₂ measure Strega
¹/₂ measure Van der Hum
   or triple sec
ice
orange or lemon peel, to dress

THESE TWO UNUSUAL LIQUEURS MAKE A VERY
AROMATIC AND FRUITY COCKTAIL.

1. Stir the gin, Strega and Van der Hum over ice and
strain into a tumbler.

2. Dress with the orange peel.

WHITE DIAMOND FRAPPÉ

SERVES 1
1/4 measure peppermint
  schnapps
1/4 measure white crème
  de cacao
1/4 measure anise liqueur
1/4 measure lemon juice
crushed ice

THIS IS A CRAZY COMBINATION OF LIQUEURS, BUT
IT WORKS WELL ONCE YOU'VE ADDED THE LEMON.
EXTRA CRUSHED ICE AT THE LAST MINUTE BRINGS OUT
ALL THE SEPARATE FLAVOURS.

1. Shake all the liquid ingredients over ice until frosted.

2. Strain into a chilled shot glass and add a small
spoonful of crushed ice.

FIRELIGHTER

SERVES 1
1 measure absinthe, iced
1 measure lime juice
    cordial, iced
ice

1. Ice a glass.

2. Shake the absinthe and lime over ice and, when well frosted, strain into the glass.

AFTER FIVE

SERVES 1
1/2 measure chilled
    peppermint schnapps
1 measure chilled
    Kahlúa
1 tbsp chilled Baileys
    Irish Cream

1. Pour the peppermint schnapps into a shot glass.

2. Carefully pour the Kahlúa over the back of a teaspoon so that it forms a separate layer.

3. Finally, float the Baileys Irish Cream on top.

TORNADO

SERVES 1
1 measure peach or
   other favourite
   schnapps, frozen
1 measure black
   Sambuca, frozen

1. Pour the schnapps into
an iced shot glass.

2. Then gently pour on the
sambuca over the back of
a spoon.

3. Leave it for a few minutes
to settle and separate
before you down it.

TOFFEE SPLIT

SERVES 1
crushed ice
2 measures Drambuie
1 measure toffee liqueur,
   iced

1. Fill a small cocktail glass
or shot glass with crushed
ice.

2. Pour on the Drambuie
and pour in the toffee
liqueur carefully from the
side of the glass so it layers
on top.

3. Drink immediately.

B52

SERVES 1
1 measure chilled dark
  crème de cacao
1 measure chilled
  Baileys Irish Cream
1 measure chilled
  Grand Marnier

THE B-52 WAS CREATED IN THE FAMOUS ALICE'S RESTAURANT IN MALIBU, CALIFORNIA. THE NAME REFERS TO THE B-52 STRATOFORTRESS LONG-RANGE BOMBER.

1. Pour the dark crème de cacao into a shot glass.

2. With a steady hand, gently pour in the chilled Baileys Irish Cream to make a second layer, then gently pour in the chilled Grand Marnier.

3. Cover and slam.

COWBOY

SERVES 1
3 measures rye whiskey
2 tbsp single cream
cracked ice

IN FILMS, COWBOYS DRINK THEIR RYE NEAT, OFTEN
PULLING THE CORK OUT OF THE BOTTLE WITH THEIR
TEETH. IT IS CERTAINLY DIFFICULT TO IMAGINE JOHN
WAYNE OR CLINT EASTWOOD SIPPING DELICATELY
FROM A CHILLED COCKTAIL GLASS.

1. Pour the whiskey and single cream over ice and
shake vigorously until well frosted.

2. Strain into a chilled glass.

PARADISE

SERVES 1
cracked ice
1 measure gin
1/2 measure apricot brandy
1/2 measure freshly squeezed
    orange juice
dash lemon juice

THIS FRUITY COMBINATION IS TRULY HEAVENLY WITH
JUST A HINT OF SHARPNESS TO PREVENT IT FROM
BECOMING SICKLY SWEET.

1. Put the ice in a cocktail shaker and pour in the gin,
apricot brandy, orange juice and lemon juice.

2. Close the shaker and shake vigorously for 10–20
seconds, until the outside of the shaker is misted.

3. Strain into a tumbler.

SANGRITA

SERVES 16
600 ml/1 pint tomato juice
300 ml/ 10 fl oz freshly squeezed
    orange juice
125 ml/4 fl oz freshly squeezed lime
    juice
1 jalapeño chilli, seeded and finely
    chopped
1 tbsp Worcestershire sauce
1 tbsp Tabasco sauce
celery salt and ground white pepper
1 bottle (775 ml/26 fl oz) tequila,
    chilled

AS YOU NEED TO MIX THE INGREDIENTS AT LEAST AN
HOUR IN ADVANCE, THIS IS THE PERFECT DRINK TO
SERVE TO GUESTS AND CLOSE FRIENDS.

1. Pour the tomato juice, orange juice and lime juice
into a large jug and stir in the chilli, Worcestershire
sauce and Tabasco sauce. Season with celery salt and
white pepper, then chill in the refrigerator for at least
one hour, or longer if you want the mixture to taste
spicier.

2. To serve, pour a measure of tequila into a shot glass
and a measure of sangrita into a second shot glass.
Drink the tequila in a single swallow, then chase with
the sangrita.

Chapter 8
Layered Lift-off

POUSSE-CAFÉ

SERVES 1
¹/₄ measure grenadine
¹/₄ measure crème de menthe
¹/₄ measure Galliano
¹/₄ measure kümmel
¹/₄ measure brandy

★ ! ▼

A POUSSE-CAFÉ IS A LAYERED COCKTAIL OF MANY DIFFERENT COLOURED LIQUEURS. IT IS CRUCIAL TO ICE ALL THE LIQUEURS FIRST.

1. Ice all the liqueurs and a tall shot, elgin or pousse-café glass.

2. Carefully pour the liqueurs over a spoon evenly into the glass.

3. Leave for a few minutes to settle.

FIFTH AVENUE

SERVES 1
1 measure dark crème de cacao,
    iced
1 measure apricot brandy, iced
1 measure cream

AFTER-DINNER COCKTAILS OFTEN INCLUDE CREAM
AND THIS ONE ALSO HAS THE DELICATE FLAVOURS OF
APRICOT AND COCOA.

1. Pour the crème de cacao into a chilled cocktail glass.
Carefully add a layer of apricot brandy over the back of
a spoon resting against the edge of the glass. Repeat
with a layer of cream. Each layer should float on top of
the previous one.

ANGEL'S DELIGHT

SERVES 1
1/2 measure chilled grenadine
1/2 measure chilled triple sec
1/2 measure chilled sloe gin
1/2 measure chilled single cream

THIS IS A MODERN VERSION OF THE CLASSIC POUSSE-CAFÉ, AN UNMIXED, MIXED DRINK, IN THAT THE INGREDIENTS FORM SEPARATE LAYERS IN THE GLASS. YOU CAN DRINK IT AS A SLAMMER OR SIP IT.

1. Pour the grenadine into a chilled shot glass or pousse-café glass, then, with a steady hand, pour in the triple sec to make a second layer.

2. Add the sloe gin to make a third layer and, finally, add the cream to float on top.

AURORA BOREALIS

SERVES 1
1 measure iced grappa or vodka
1 measure iced green Chartreuse
1/2 measure iced orange curaçao
few drops iced cassis

LIKE A POUSSE-CAFÉ, THIS SPECTACULAR COLOURED
DRINK SHOULD NOT BE MIXED OR STIRRED. LEAVE
IT TO SWIRL AROUND THE GLASS, CREATING A
MULTIHUED EFFECT AND TRY TO GUESS THE VARIOUS
FLAVOURS.

1. Pour the grappa slowly around one side of a well-
chilled shot glass.

2. Gently pour the Chartreuse around the other side.

3. Pour the curaçao gently into the middle and add
a few drops of cassis just before serving. Don't stir.
Drink slowly!

NAPOLEON'S NIGHTCAP

SERVES 1
1¼ measures cognac
1 measure dark crème de cacao
¼ measure crème de banane
ice
1 tbsp cream

INSTEAD OF HOT CHOCOLATE, NAPOLEON FAVOURED
A CHOCOLATE-LACED BRANDY WITH A HINT OF
BANANA. DARING AND EXTRAVAGANT!

1. Stir the cognac, crème de cacao and crème de
banane in a mixing glass with ice.

2. Strain into a chilled glass and spoon on a layer
of cream.

STARS AND SWIRLS

SERVES 1
1 measure Malibu
large ice cube
1/2 measure strawberry
   or raspberry liqueur
1 tsp blue curaçao

1. Chill a small shot glass really well.

2. Pour in the Malibu and add a large ice cube.

3. Carefully pour in the strawberry liqueur and blue curaçao from opposite sides of the glass very slowly so they fall down the sides and swirl around.

FANCY FREE

SERVES 1
1/3 measure cherry
   brandy, iced
1/3 measure Cointreau,
   iced
1/3 measure apricot
   liqueur, iced

1. Pour the three liqueurs into an iced tall shot glass, one at a time, in the order listed. Pour each one over the back of a spoon to form layers.

NUCLEAR FALLOUT

SERVES 1
1 tsp raspberry syrup
1/4 measure maraschino
    liqueur
1/4 measure yellow
    Chartreuse
1/4 measure Cointreau
1/2 measure well-iced
    blue curaçao

1. Chill all the liqueurs but put the blue curaçao in the coldest part of the freezer. Also chill a shot or pousse-café glass.

2. Carefully pour each liqueur except the blue curaçao in layers over the back of a teaspoon.

3. Finally, pour in the blue curaçao and wait for the fallout!

CAPUCINE

SERVES 1
crushed ice
1 measure iced blue
    curaçao
1 measure iced parfait
    amour

1. Pack a small cocktail or shot glass with finely crushed ice.

2. Pour in the curaçao slowly and then carefully top up with the parfait amour.

BANANA BOMBER

SERVES 1
1 measure crème de
  banane
1 measure brandy

THIS COCKTAIL IS AS DAZZLING AS IT IS DELICIOUS
AND GLORIOUSLY ADDICTIVE. TRY IT WITH WHITE
CRÈME DE CACAO AND A LAYER OF CREAM TOO –
EQUALLY IRRESISTIBLE!

1. Pour the banana liqueur gently into a shot glass.

2. Gently pour in the brandy over the back of a
teaspoon, taking care not to let the layers mix.

AFRICAN MINT

SERVES 1
3/4 measure crème de menthe, chilled
3/4 measure Amarula, chilled

AMARULA IS A VERY RICH AND EXOTIC LIQUEUR THAT IS BEST SERVED AND DRUNK REALLY COLD – BUT NOT ON ICE, AS THAT WOULD DILUTE ITS REAL CHARACTER.

1. Pour the crème de menthe into the bottom of a slim cocktail glass or shot glass, saving a few drops.

2. Pour the Amarula slowly over the back of a spoon to create a layer over the mint.

3. Drizzle any remaining drops of mint over the creamy liqueur to finish.

Chapter 9
The Perfect Shot

SPUTNIK

SERVES 1
1 measure vodka
1 measure single cream
1 tsp maraschino liqueur
ice
maraschino cherry, to dress

IF YOU ARE MAKING SEVERAL OF THESE THEY CAN BE PREPARED IN ADVANCE WITH DIFFERENT COLOURED CHERRIES IN ORBIT ON TOP.

1. Shake all the liquid ingredients over ice and strain into a glass.

2. Dress with the cherry supported on two or more crossed cocktail sticks.

PERFECT LOVE

SERVES 1
1 measure vodka
1/2 measure parfait amour
1/2 measure maraschino liqueur
crushed ice

THIS IS THE LITERAL TRANSLATION FOR AN UNUSUAL PURPLE LIQUEUR FLAVOURED WITH ROSE PETALS, ALMONDS AND VANILLA.

1. Shake all the liquid ingredients together over ice until frosted.

2. Strain into a chilled tall thin glass with more ice.

DEPTH CHARGE

SERVES 1
1 measure gin
1 measure Lillet
2 dashes Pernod
ice

ANISE IS A PARTICULARLY UNUSUAL DRINK IN THAT IT TURNS CLOUDY WHEN MIXED WITH WATER BUT NOT WHEN MIXED WITH OTHER ALCOHOLIC DRINKS, UNTIL THE ICE STARTS MELTING.

1. Shake all the liquid ingredients over ice until well frosted.

2. Strain into a chilled glass.

PEACH FLOYD

SERVES 1
1 measure peach schnapps, chilled
1 measure vodka, chilled
1 measure white cranberry and peach
   juice, chilled
1 measure cranberry juice, chilled
ice

SHOTS LOOK STUNNING IN THE RIGHT TYPE OF GLASS,
BUT AS THEY ARE FOR DRINKING DOWN IN ONE, KEEP
THEM SMALL AND HAVE EVERYTHING REALLY WELL
CHILLED.

1. Stir all the liquid ingredients together over ice and
pour into an iced shot glass.

JEALOUSY

SERVES 1
1 tsp crème de menthe
1–2 tbsp double cream
2 measures coffee or chocolate liqueur
chocolate matchsticks, to serve

THIS REALLY IS AN AFTER-DINNER COCKTAIL AND IF
YOU WANT A CHANGE, YOU COULD FLAVOUR THE
CREAM WITH A DIFFERENT LIQUEUR.

1. Gently beat the mint liqueur into the cream until
thick.

2. Pour the coffee liqueur into a very small iced glass
and carefully spoon on the whipped flavoured cream.

3. Serve with the chocolate matchsticks.

ALASKA

SERVES 1
1/2 measure gin
1/2 measure yellow
   Chartreuse
ice

1. Shake the liquid ingredients over ice until well frosted.

2. Strain into a chilled glass.

BREAKFAST

SERVES 1
2 measures gin
1 measure grenadine
cracked ice
1 egg yolk

1. Pour the gin and grenadine over ice in a shaker and add the egg yolk.

2. Shake vigorously until frosted. Strain into a chilled glass.

PEPPERMINT PATTY

SERVES 1
cracked ice
1 measure white crème
   de cacao
1 measure white crème
   de menthe

1. Put the ice in a cocktail shaker and pour in the crème de cacao and crème de menthe.

2. Close the shaker and shake vigorously for 10–20 seconds, until the outside of the shaker is misted.

3. Strain into a shot glass.

ZIPPER

SERVES 1
crushed ice
1 measure tequila
1/2 measure Grand
   Marnier
1/2 measure single cream

1. Put the crushed ice into a cocktail shaker and pour in the tequila, Grand Marnier and cream.

2. Close the shaker and shake vigorously for 10–20 seconds, until the outside of the shaker is misted.

3. Strain into a shot glass.

TEQUILA SHOT

SERVES 1
1 measure gold tequila
pinch salt
lime wedge

ACCORDING TO CUSTOM THIS IS THE ONLY WAY TO
DRINK NEAT TEQUILA. IT IS OFTEN DESCRIBED AS BEING
SMOOTH AND TART, SO ADDING LIME JUICE AND SALT
MAY SOUND CONTRADICTORY, BUT IT WORKS!

1. Pour the tequila into a shot glass.

2. Put the salt at the base of your thumb, between your
thumb and forefinger.

3. Hold the lime wedge in the same hand.

4. Hold the shot in the other hand.

5. Lick the salt, down the tequila and suck the lime.

VOODOO

SERVES 1
1/2 measure chilled Kahlúa
1/2 measure chilled Malibu
1/2 measure chilled
   butterscotch schnapps
1 measure chilled milk

THIS ENTHRALLING MIXTURE OF FLAVOURS IS
GUARANTEED TO WEAVE A SPELL ON YOUR TASTE
BUDS AND WORK ITS MAGIC FROM THE VERY FIRST SIP.

1. Pour the Kahlúa, Malibu, schnapps and milk into a
glass and stir well.

WHISKEY SOUR JELLY SHOT

SERVES 8
1 packet lemon gelatine
1/2 cup hot water
3/4–1 cup bourbon whiskey

A NEW TWIST ON A CLASSIC COCKTAIL FOR A NEW GENERATION OF COCKTAIL DRINKERS, BUT BE CAREFUL TO KEEP CHILDREN AWAY FROM THE REFRIGERATOR.

1. Place the gelatine in a large heatproof measuring cup or jug. Pour in the hot water and stir until the gelatine has dissolved.

2. Let cool, then stir in the whiskey to make the mixture up to 475 ml/16 fl oz.

3. Divide among eight shot glasses or small paper cups and chill in the refrigerator until set. If using paper cups, transfer the jelly shots to shot glasses before serving.

MARGARITA JELLY SHOT

SERVES 10
1/2 lime, cut into wedges
2 tbsp fine salt
1 packet lime gelatine
300 ml/10 fl oz hot water
4–5 tbsp Cointreau
200–250 ml/7–9 fl oz tequila

IT IS NOT ESSENTIAL TO FROST THE GLASSES WITH SALT
BUT IT DOES LOOK ATTRACTIVE AND PAYS HOMAGE TO
THE ORIGINAL NON-JELLY COCKTAIL RECIPE OF 1942.

1. Rub the outside rims of 10 shot glasses with the lime
wedges, then dip in the salt to frost them. Set aside.

2. Place the gelatine in a large heatproof measuring
jug. Pour in the hot water and stir until the gelatine has
dissolved. Let cool, then stir in the Cointreau and tequila
to make the mixture up to 475 ml/16 fl oz.

3. Divide among the prepared shot glasses, taking
care not to disturb the salt frosting and chill in the
refrigerator until set.

Chapter 10

Keeping a Clear Head

SHIRLEY TEMPLE

SERVES 1
2 measures lemon juice
1 1/2 measure grenadine
1/2 measure sugar syrup
cracked ice
ginger ale
orange slice and cocktail
    cherry, to dress

THE SHIRLEY TEMPLE IS ONE OF THE MOST FAMOUS NON-ALCOHOLIC DRINKS – THIS CLASSIC IS NAMED AFTER THE VERY POPULAR 1930S CHILD FILM STAR.

1. Shake the lemon juice, grenadine and sugar syrup vigorously over ice cubes until well frosted.

2. Half-fill a small, chilled highball glass with cracked ice and strain the liquid into it.

3. Fill with ginger ale and dress with a slice of orange.

FAUX KIR ROYALE

SERVES 1
4–6 ice cubes, cracked
1½ measures raspberry syrup
sparkling apple juice, chilled

LOOKS JUST LIKE THE REAL THING, BUT WON'T GET YOU INTO A RIGHT ROYAL STATE.

1. Put the cracked ice into a mixing glass and pour the raspberry syrup over it.

2. Stir well to mix, then strain into a wine glass.

3. Fill with chilled sparkling apple juice and stir.

ST CLEMENTS

SERVES 1
cracked ice
2 measures fresh orange juice
2 measures bitter lemon
orange slice, to dress
lemon slice, to dress

ANYONE FAMILIAR WITH THE NURSERY RHYME WILL
KNOW IMMEDIATELY WHAT THE INGREDIENTS OF THIS
REFRESHING DRINK ARE.

1. Put the cracked ice into a chilled highball glass.

2. Pour in the orange juice and bitter lemon.

3. Stir gently and dress with a slice of orange and
a slice of lemon.

FRUIT COOLER

SERVES 2
250 ml/8 fl oz orange juice
125 ml/4 fl oz natural yogurt
2 eggs
2 bananas, sliced and frozen
fresh banana slices, to dress

THIS IS A GREAT BREAKFAST ENERGIZER AND GIVES YOU A HEALTHY START TO THE DAY, ONCE YOU'VE HAD YOUR WORKOUT.

1. Pour the orange juice and yogurt into a food processor and process gently until combined.

2. Add the eggs and frozen bananas and process until smooth.

3. Pour the mixture into highball or hurricane glasses and dress the rims with slices of fresh banana.

BRIGHT GREEN COOLER

SERVES 1
3 measures pineapple juice
2 measures lime juice
1 measure green peppermint syrup
cracked ice
ginger ale
cucumber twist, to dress
lime slice, to dress

MORE LIGHT THAN BRIGHT, BUT DEFINITELY COOL

1. Shake the pineapple juice, lime juice and green peppermint syrup vigorously over ice cubes until well frosted.

2. Half-fill a tall chilled highball glass with the cracked ice and strain the cocktail over it.

3. Fill with ginger ale and dress with the cucumber and lime.

BABY BELLINI

SERVES 1
2 measures peach juice
1 measure lemon juice
sparkling apple juice

1. Pour the peach juice and lemon juice into a chilled champagne flute and stir well.

2. Fill with sparkling apple juice and stir again.

NON-ALCOHOLIC PIMM'S

SERVES 6
600 ml/1 pint lemonade, chilled
450 ml/15 fl oz cola, chilled
450 ml/15 fl oz dry ginger ale, chilled
juice of 1 orange
juice of 1 lemon
a few drops of Angostura bitters
fruit slices
mint sprigs
ice cubes

1. Mix the lemonade, cola, dry ginger ale, orange juice, lemon juice and bitters together in a large jug or punch bowl.

2. Float in the fruit slices and mint, store in a cold place and add ice cubes at the last minute.

3. Serve in chilled highball glasses for a cooling effect.

SLUSH PUPPY

SERVES 1
ice cubes
juice of 1 lemon or 1/2 pink
  grapefruit
1 1/2 measures grenadine
2–3 lemon peel strips
2–3 tsp raspberry syrup
soda water
1 maraschino cherry

1. Fill a highball glass with ice cubes and pour in the lemon juice and grenadine.

2. Add the lemon peel, syrup and soda water to taste and dress with the cherry.

VIRGIN MARY

SERVES 1
3 measures tomato juice
1 measure lemon juice
2 dashes Worcestershire
  sauce
1 dash Tabasco sauce
cracked ice
celery salt
black pepper
lemon wedge, to dress
celery stalk, to dress

1. Shake the tomato juice, lemon juice, Worcestershire sauce and Tabasco vigorously over cracked ice and season with celery salt and black pepper.

2. Strain into an iced old-fashioned or lowball glass and dress with the lemon and celery.

INDEX

A

Absinthe
   Firelighter 90
Adam and Eve 47
African Mint 105
After Five 90
Alabama Slammer 87
Alaska 112
Amaretto
   Alabama Slammer 87
   Godmother 60
   Ocean Breeze 35
Amarula
   African Mint 105
   Vodka Espresso 75
Angel's Delight 99
Anise liqueur see also
   Pernod; Sambuca
   White Diamond Frappé
   89
Anouchka 59
Apple Classic 45
Apple Martini 79
Apricot liqueur
   Fancy Free 102
Aurora Borealis 100

B

B-52 92
Baby Bellini 124
Baileys Irish Cream
   After Five 90
   B-52 92
   Brain Haemorrhage 85
   Mudslide 34
Banana Bomber 104
Bellini 27
Bellinitini 63
Black Beauty 64
Black Russian 58
Black Widow 32
Bloody Mary 53
Blue Lagoon 55
Blue Monday 65
The Blues 41
Brain Haemorrhage 85
Brandy
   Apple Classic 45
   Banana Bomber 104
   Cherry Kitch 48
   Deauville Passion 46

Fancy Free 102
Fifth Avenue 98
Napoleon's Nightcap 101
Paradise 94
Peartini 67
Pousse-Café 97
Singapore Sling 22
Breakfast 112
Bright Green Cooler 123
Bullshot 80

C

Calvados
   Apple Classic 45
Capucine 103
Champagne
   Bellini 27
   Bellinitini 63
   Flirtini 81
   Mimosa 22
Charleston 42
Chartreuse
   Alaska 112
   Aurora Borealis 100
   Nuclear Fallout 103
Cherry Kitch 48
Chocolate liqueur see also
   Crème de cacao
   Jealousy 111
Chocolate Martini 79
Cider
   Apple Classic 45
Club Mojito 24
Coffee liqueur see also
   Kahlúa
   Black Russian 58
   Jealousy 111
Cognac
   Deauville Passion 46
   Napoleon's Nightcap 101
Cointreau
   Blue Monday 65
   Charleston 42
   Fancy Free 102
   Flirtini 81
   Margarita 20
   Margarita Jelly Shot 117
   Nuclear Fallout 103
   Silver Berry 83
   White Cosmopolitan 40
Cosmopolitan 51

Cowboy 93
Cranberry Collins 82
Crème de banane
   Banana Bomber 104
   Napoleon's Nightcap 101
Crème de cacao
   B-52 92
   Chocolate Martini 79
   Fifth Avenue 98
   Flying Grasshopper 76
   Jealousy 111
   Napoleon's Nightcap 101
   Peppermint Patty 113
   Pink Squirrel 43
   White Diamond Frappé
   89
Crème de cassis
   Silver Berry 83
Crème de framboise
   Metropolitan 73
Crème de menthe
   African Mint 105
   Flying Grasshopper 76
   Jealousy 111
   Long Island Iced Tea 57
   Peppermint Patty 113
   Pousse-Café 97
Crème de mure
   Anouchka 59
Crème de noyaux
   Pink Squirrel 43
Curaçao
   Aurora Borealis 100
   Black Widow 32
   Blue Lagoon 55
   Blue Monday 65
   The Blues 41
   Capucine 103
   Deauville Passion 46
   Island Blues 94
   Mai Tai 21
   Mimosa 22
   Nuclear Fallout 103
   Ocean Breeze 35
   Stars and Swirls 102

D

Daiquiri 26
Deauville Passion 46
Depth Charge 109
Drambuie

Toffee Split 91
Dry Martini 23

F
Fancy Free 102
Faux Kir Royale 120

Fifth Avenue 98
Firelighter 90
Flirtini 81
Flying Grasshopper 76
Fraise liqueur
    Strawberrini 69
Fruit Cocktail 122
Fuzzy Navel 68

G
Galliano
    Golden Frog 69
    Harvey Wallbanger 56
    Pousse-Café 97
Gin
    Alabama Slammer 87
    Alaska 112
    Angel's Delight 99
    Apple Classic 45
    Breakfast 112
    Charleston 42
    Depth Charge 109
    Dry Martini 23
    High Flyer 88
    Indian Summer 35
    Long Island Iced Tea 57
    Martinez 49
    Martini 17
    Moonlight 44
    Orange Blossom 45
    Palm Beach 36
    Paradise 94
    Singapore Sling 22
    Slow Comfortable Screw
        56
    White Lady 30
Ginger beer
    Moscow Mule 66
Godmother 60
Golden Frog 69
Grand Marnier
    B-52 92
    Zipper 113
Grappa
    Aurora Borealis 100
Greyhound 78

H
Harvey Wallbanger 56
High Flyer 88
Hurricane 23

I
Indian Summer 35
Island Blues 34

J
Japanese Slipper 57
Jealousy 111

K
Kahlúa
    After Five 90
    Indian Summer 35
    Mudslide 34
    Voodoo 115
Kamikaze 31
Kirsch
    Charleston 42
    Cherry Kitch 48
    Moonlight 44
Kümmel
    Pousse-Café 97

L
Lillet
    Depth Charge 109
Limoncello
    White Cosmopolitan 40
Long Island Iced Tea 57

M
Mai Tai 21
Malibu
    Stars and Swirls 102
    Voodoo 115
Manhattan 18
Maraschino liqueur
    The Blues 41
    Charleston 42
    Martinez 49
    Nuclear Fallout 103
    Perfect Love 108
    Sputnik 107
Margarita 20
Margarita Jelly Shot 117
Martinez 49
Martini 17
Metropolitan 73
Midori
    Japanese Slipper 57
Mimi 78

Mimosa 22
Mint Julep 29
Moonlight 44
Moscow Mule 66
Mudslide 34

N
Napoleon's Nightcap 101
Nirvana 33
Non-alcoholic cocktails
    Baby Bellini 124
    Bright Green Cooler 123
    Faux Kir Royale 120
    Fruit Cocktail 122
    Non-alcoholic Pimms
        124
    Shirley Temple 119
    Slush Puppy 125
    St Clements 121
    Virgin Mary 125
    Nuclear Fallout 103

O
Ocean Breeze 35
Orange Blossom 45

P
Palm Beach 36
Paradise 94
Parfait Amour
    Capucine 103
    Perfect Love 108
Peach Floyd 110
Peartini 67
Peppermint Patty 113
Perfect Love 108
Pernod
    Depth Charge 109
    Zombie 39
Piña Colada 19
Pink Squirrel 43
Pousse-Café 97
Purple Passion 77

R
Raspberry liqueur
    Stars and Swirls 102
Red wine
    Sangria 25
Rum
    Black Widow 32
    Club Mojito 24
    Daiquiri 26
    Hurricane 23
    Long Island Iced Tea 57

Mai Tai 21
Nirvana 33
Ocean Breeze 35
Palm Beach 36
Piña Colada 19
Spotted Bikini 68
Zombie 39
Russian Double 61

S
Salty Dog 70
Sambuca
Anouchka 59
Black Beauty 64
Tornado 91
Zander 44
Sangria 25
Sangrita 95
Schnapps
After Five 90
Apple Martini 79
Bellinitini 63
Brain Haemorrhage 85
Fuzzy Navel 68
Island Blues 34
Peach Floyd 110
Russian Double 61
Sex on the Beach 52
Tornado 91
Voodoo 115
White Diamond Frappé 8
Woo-Woo 71
Screwdriver 54
Sex on the Beach 52
Sherry
Bloody Mary 53
Shirley Temple 119
Silver Berry 83
Singapore Sling 22
Slow Comfortable Screw 56
Slush Puppy 125
Southern Comfort
Alabama Slammer 87
Black Widow 32
Spotted Bikini 68
Sputnik 107
Stars and Swirls 102
Strawberrini 69
Strega
Golden Frog 69
High Flyer 88
St Clements 121

T
Tequila
The Blues 41
Long Island Iced Tea 57
Margarita 20
Margarita Jelly Shot 117
Sangria 95
Tequila Shot 114
Tequila Slammer 86
Zipper 113
Tequila Slammer 86
Toffee Split 91
Tornado 91
Triple sec
Adam and Eve 47
Angel's Delight 99
Cosmopolitan 51
High Flyer 88
Kamikaze 31
Margarita 20
White Lady 30
Zombie 39

V
Van der Hum
High Flyer 88
Vermouth
Charleston 42
Dry Martini 23
Manhattan 18
Martinez 49
Martini 17
Vodkatini 74
Virgin Mary 125
Vodka
Adam and Eve 47
Anouchka 59
Apple Martini 79
Aurora Borealis 100
Bellinitini 63
Black Beauty 64
Black Russian 58
Bloody Mary 53
Blue Lagoon 55
Blue Monday 65
Bullshot 80
Chocolate Martini 79
Cosmopolitan 51
Cranberry Collins 82
Flirtini 81
Flying Grasshopper 76
Fuzzy Navel 68
Godmother 60
Golden Frog 69

Greyhound 78
Harvey Wallbanger 56
Indian Summer 35
Japanese Slipper 57
Kamikaze 31
Long Island Iced Tea 57
Metropolitan 73
Mimi 78
Moscow Mule 66
Mudslide 34
Peach Floyd 110
Peartini 67
Perfect Love 108
Purple Passion 77
Russian Double 61
Salty Dog 70
Screwdriver 54
Sex on the Beach 52
Silver Berry 83
Spotted Bikini 68
Sputnik 107
Strawberrini 69
Vodka Espresso 75
Vodkatini 74
Woo-Woo 71
Vodka Espresso 75
Vodkatini 74
Voodoo 115

W
Whisky/Whiskey
Cowboy 93
Manhattan 18
Mint Julep 29
Whiskey Sour Jelly Shot 116
Whisky Sour 37
White Cosmopolitan 40
White Diamond Frappé 89
White Lady 30
White wine
Flirtini 81
Kamikaze 31
Moonlight 44
Tequila Slammer 86
Woo-Woo 71

Z
Zander 44
Zipper 113
Zombie 39

NOTES

....
....
....
....
....
....
....
....
....
....
....
....

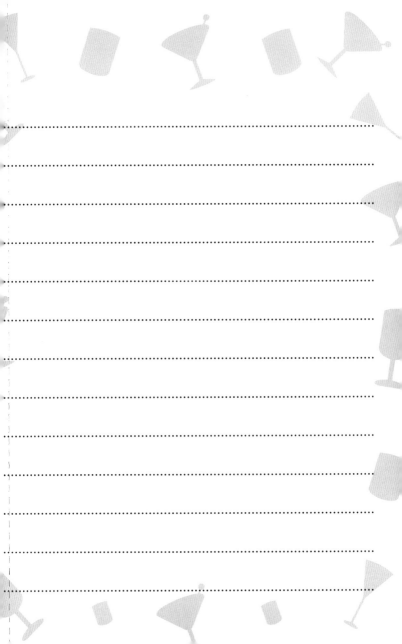

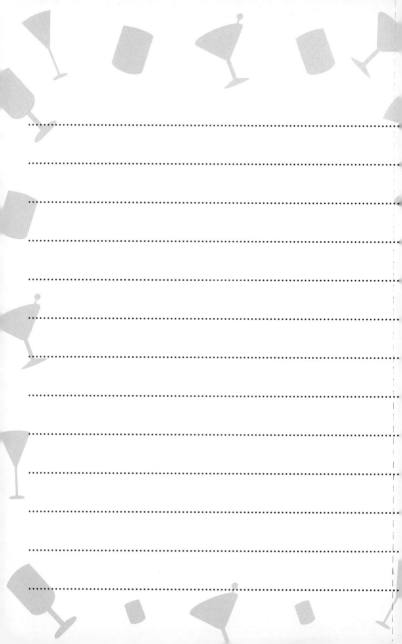

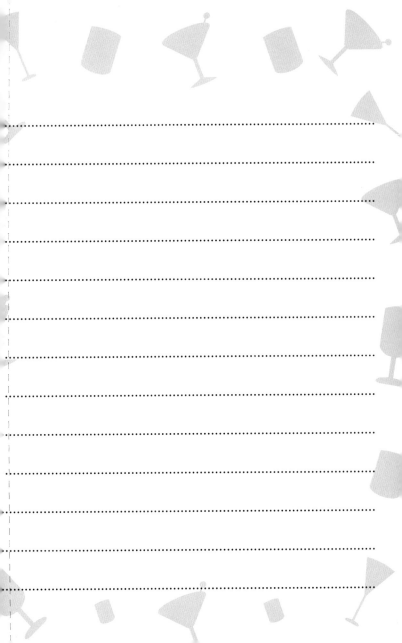

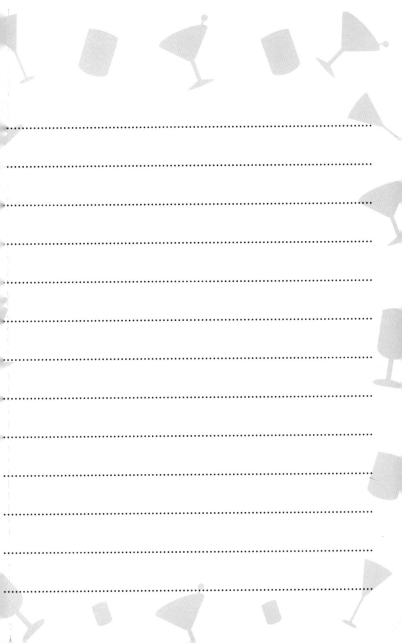

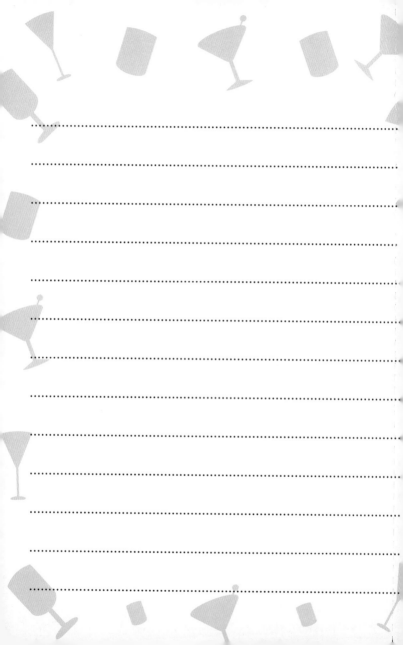

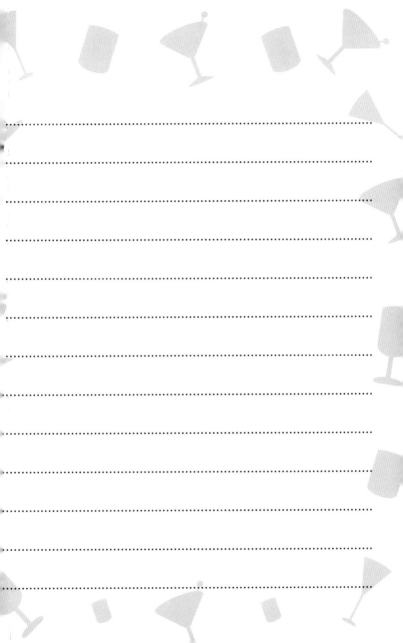

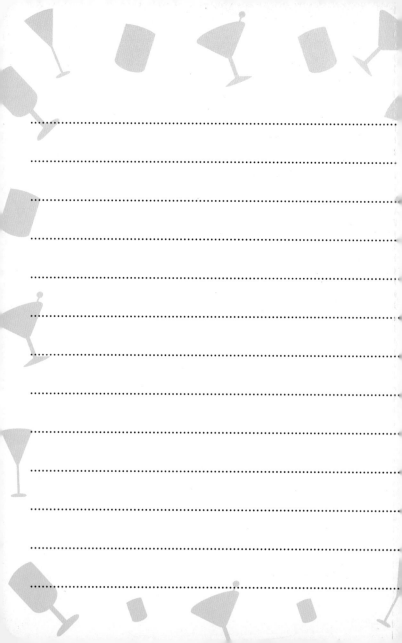